21st Century Issues

WORLD HUNGER

Steven Maddocks

WORLD ALMANAC® LIBRARY

Please visit our web site at: www.worldalmanaclibrary.com
For a free color catalog describing World Almanac® Library's list of high-quality books
and multimedia programs, call 1-800-848-2928 (USA) or 1-800-387-3178 (Canada).
World Almanac® Library's fax: (414) 332-3567.

Library of Congress Cataloging-in-Publication Data

Maddocks, Steven.
    World hunger / by Steven Maddocks.
        p. cm. — (21st century issues)
    Includes bibliographical references and index.
    ISBN 0-8368-5646-5 (lib. bdg.)
    ISBN 0-8368-5663-5 (softcover)
    1. Food supply—Juvenile literature. 2. Hunger—Juvenile literature. 3. Poverty—Juvenile
literature. 4. Food relief—Juvenile literature. I. Title. II. Series.
HD9000.5.M24 2004
338.1'9—dc22   2004042005

This North American edition first published in 2005 by
World Almanac® Library
330 West Olive Street, Suite 100
Milwaukee, WI 53212 USA

This U.S. copyright © 2005 by World Almanac® Library. Original edition copyright © 2004
by Arcturus Publishing Limited.

Series concept: Alex Woolf
Project editor: Kelly Davis
Designer: Paul Turner, Stonecastle Graphics
Consultant: Kaye Stearman
Picture researcher: Shelley Noronha, Glass Onion Pictures
World Almanac® Library editor: Carol Ryback
World Almanac® Library designer: Kami Koenig

Photo credits:
Camera Press: Benoit Gysembergh 32.
Exile Images: J. Holmes 8, 38; R. Chalasani 11; H. Davies 15, 16, 17; A. Ilic 18. Popperfoto: Danilo Krstanovic
23. Still Pictures: 20, 41; Pieternella Pieterse title page, 12; Heine Pedersen 7; Jorgen Schytte 21, 40, 45;
J. Frebet 26; Andrew Davies 31, 35; Adrian Arbib 36; Penny Tweedie 37. The Image Works: 28, 43; Steve and
Mary Skjold 9; Kathy McLaughlin 10, 13, 19, 24; Journal-Courier/Steve Warmowski 25, 27; Bob Daemmrich
29; Sean Sprague 39. Topham: cover, 4.

Printed in Italy

1 2 3 4 5 6 7 8 9 08 07 06 05 04

Cover: A young child's swollen belly is a sign of malnutrition.

CONTENTS

1: WHO IS HUNGRY?

Most readers (and the writer) of this book will never experience true hunger—a need for food so profound that it destroys mind and body. Yet in 2002, six-and-a-half million babies and young children (18,000 a day) died from hunger-related causes. In the last 30 seconds, about the time it took you to read this paragraph, five children died of hunger.

Why is this happening when we have more than enough food to feed everyone in the world and more than enough money to pay for it? Unfortunately, the food and money are not equally distributed. A small portion of the global population has more food than it needs, while the majority seldom has enough.

At the 1996 World Food Summit in Rome, Italy, 158 countries signed a pledge to halve the number of hungry people in the world by 2015. Progress is slow, but thanks to the efforts of governments, companies, aid organizations, and dedicated individuals around the world, millions of people are saved

This young child's swollen belly is a sign of malnutrition.

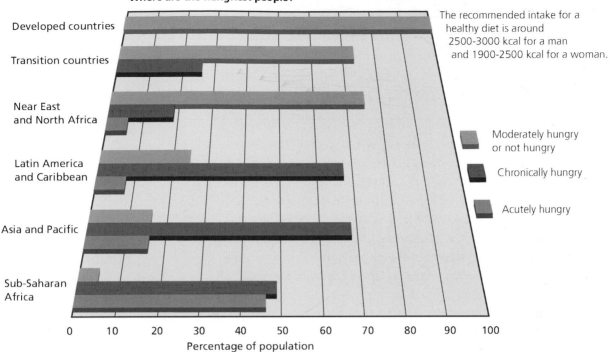

Where are the hungriest people?

The recommended intake for a healthy diet is around 2500-3000 kcal for a man and 1900-2500 kcal for a woman.

Developed countries
Transition countries
Near East and North Africa
Latin America and Caribbean
Asia and Pacific
Sub-Saharan Africa

Moderately hungry or not hungry

Chronically hungry

Acutely hungry

Percentage of population

0 10 20 30 40 50 60 70 80 90 100

Based on a graph in 'The state of food insecurity in the world', 2000, Food and Agriculture Organization website.

from starvation every year. With an even greater effort, world hunger could be reduced and even eliminated sooner.

This chapter explains some of the facts and figures related to world hunger. Chapter 2 discusses the causes of world hunger. Chapter 3 analyzes how food is produced and traded around the world. Chapter 4 examines what steps the different countries are taking to combat hunger, and Chapter 5 explores what the future holds.

Acute versus chronic hunger

Over the last twenty years, several food emergencies occurred. Television images showing large numbers of skeletally thin people starving to death became familiar and even commonplace. Starvation such as this is called acute hunger. The diet of a person suffering from acute hunger is deficient in everything—his or her body is simply not getting enough food. The daily energy intake of an acutely hungry person is lower than the recommended amount by 400 Calories or more. Yet acute hunger accounts for only 10 percent of hunger deaths. The other 90 percent die a much slower death from chronic hunger (malnutrition), which attracts far fewer headlines.

This graph illustrates the severity of hunger in the regions of the world. The mauve bar represents the percentage of the population that is moderately hungry or not hungry; the dark blue bar represents the percentage that is chronically hungry; and the light blue bar represents the percentage that is acutely hungry.

PERSPECTIVES

"If the food currently available were to be evenly and equitably distributed among the 6.4 billion people on the planet, there would still be a surplus left for 800 million people."

Devinder Sharma, award-winning Indian journalist and author on food and trade policy, writing in the United Kingdom's Guardian newspaper, August 22, 2002

The diet of a chronically hungry person is 100–400 Calories a day less than the recommended intake. While this deficit is not usually enough to kill a person quickly, the body reacts to this gradual starvation by slowing down physical activity, mental development, and growth. Even simple tasks seem overwhelming. Concentration in school or at work becomes exhausting and difficult. The immune system weakens, turning simple colds into severe pneumonia; diarrhea may lead to dangerous dysentery. Those who survive remain damaged for life. If they have children, parenthood is a great struggle, and their children will likely suffer similar hardships. Millions of people in poor, rural communities become trapped in this repeating cycle of hunger.

Three-quarters of those who die of hunger every year are under the age of five. Hunger is a larger problem for children than adults because younger people are more dependent on a good diet to remain healthy and to grow properly. Children are also less able to fend for themselves. They rely on others (their parents, school, or community) to provide their food. Children generally suffer the worst effects during a food shortage.

Where are the hungry people?

In 2002, the Food and Agriculture Organization of the United Nations (FAO) estimated that 840 million people in the world were hungry. About 799 million (95 percent of the total) lived in developing countries, the poorest group of countries, whose economies are based mainly on agriculture. The developed countries, also known as the industrialized nations because of their industrial economies and high standards of living, accounted for 11 million. The remaining 30 million lived in countries whose economies were in transition. These were mainly Eastern European countries such as Albania and Bulgaria, and former Soviet republics such as Armenia and Kazakhstan.

By numbers, hunger affects the most people in Asia, with 233 million undernourished people in India and 119 million in China. These numbers are falling (particularly in China), and most hungry people in Asia suffer from what is considered a moderate level of undernourishment—an average daily deficit of about 200 Calories. If hunger is measured by the percentage of the population affected, then sub-Saharan Africa (the part of Africa south of the Sahara Desert) is by far the worst region in the world, with as many as 70 percent of the people in some countries going hungry. And, African hunger is more severe, with a much lower average daily intake of calories than in Asia.

Rising populations in the affected countries make combating hunger and poverty more difficult. Asia's population doubled in the last forty years, and Africa's population has tripled. The United Nations estimates that, if the world's population continues to rise as expected, by the year 2050, nine out of ten people will live in a developing country.

Hundreds of people line up for emergency food aid in the desert heat of drought-stricken Ethiopia in Africa.

CASE STUDY

Samira Khan lives in an isolated village in the hills of Pakistan. She is fifteen and newly married. She lives with her husband's family. The men work all day on a nearby plantation, where sugarcane is grown—for sale overseas. During the day, Samira looks after the house. She fetches water from a well about two miles away, washes clothes, and prepares the meals. Although she looks quite healthy, she is malnourished.

In the morning, Samira drinks tea with milk and sugar and gives the men their breakfast. When they have left, Samira eats her share—one paratha (a type of pancake made of flour and butter). Sometimes she has a fried egg. In the afternoon she eats a chapati, a type of bread, with vegetables and sometimes beans. In the evening, Samira serves the men their meal and then eats hers: another chapati with vegetables.

The village is a long way from any towns, and Samira's husband has very little money. Samira depends on what she can grow for food. Her diet is deficient in fats and carbohydrates, and she needs more vitamins, calcium, and iron. Samira is still young; if her diet does not improve, her body and mind will not develop healthily. If she becomes pregnant, her health and that of her baby will be at risk.

Young girls study in northern Pakistan in 1998.

What is malnutrition?

Malnutrition is ongoing chronic hunger that either gradually kills sufferers or causes them permanent health damage. Malnourished people do not generally appear emaciated (so thin they look like skin and bones), so it's hard to identify a malnourished person by looking at him or her. For this

reason, malnutrition is sometimes called the "hidden hunger."
Malnutrition is also known as the "silent emergency,"
because—compared with dramatic stories of unforeseen
food emergencies—it attracts little media attention. Mildly
to moderately malnourished children, who simply fall ill and
never recover, account for three-quarters of malnutrition deaths
throughout the world.

Malnutrition is especially hard on children up to age three and
pregnant women and their unborn babies. Children who suffer
malnutrition remain damaged for life in body and mind. If
a pregnant mother is malnourished (or if she experienced
malnutrition during her own childhood),
she will likely give birth to an
underweight baby, weakened for life.

Malnutrition is not just a problem of
the developing world. During the 1990s,
a U.S. congressional study found that
for at least part of the month (usually
in the week before payday) one in nine
Americans cannot afford to feed
themselves adequately. In November
2003, a panel of British nutrition experts
found that two million people in England,
including up to 60 percent of people
arriving for hospital treatment, were
undernourished.

Volunteers at a church soup
kitchen in Minneapolis serve
Christmas dinner.

An age-old problem

In early human history, societies depended on
small-scale agriculture, hunting, herding, and fishing
to supply their food. (While this is no longer true in
industrialized countries, people in many nations still farm
or hunt their own food.) Agricultural communities often suffer
a severe food shortage if livestock die or a harvest fails.

Famine (a severe food shortage) occurred frequently in ancient
times. An Egyptian stela (engraved stone pillar) dating from
about 2760 B.C. describes a seven-year famine caused by a
drought that left farmlands bordering the Nile River parched.
The inscription recalls that "children cried. . . . The hearts of
the old were needy. . . . Temples were shut, shrines covered
with dust, everyone was in distress."

From 1845 to 1849, a potato famine in Ireland, caused by a combination of crop disease and inadequate relief efforts, reduced that country's population by about 25 percent. During the First World War (1914–1918), entire communities, particularly in Eastern Europe and Russia, were uprooted by the fighting and forced to flee their homes. This internal refugee crisis was made worse by a devastating drought in 1921. The resulting general famine that followed killed between two and ten million Russians.

People line up for bread in war-ravaged St. Petersburg, Russia, in 1917.

What is being done about world hunger?

The United Nations (UN) was founded on October 24, 1945, after the end of World War II (1939–1945)—which had caused even greater devastation than World War I. One of the UN's priorities was helping people who faced starvation as a result of the war, so the UN immediately established the Food and Agriculture Organization (FAO). In 1962, the UN established the World Food Program (WFP), which distributes food aid. The WFP—the world's largest food organization—delivers more than 7 million tons (6.5 million tonnes) of food annually. In 2002, the WFP fed about 72 million people in 82 countries.

As the number of hungry people in the world began escalating rapidly during the 1970s, a great many individuals, companies,

PERSPECTIVES

"Hunger persists because hungry people lack the opportunity they need to bring their own hunger to an end. Only by mobilizing the energy, responsibility, creativity, and resources of the poor themselves can a society be created that is truly free from hunger."

The Hunger Project, a global movement based in New York that campaigns for an end to world hunger. (www.thp.org)

and organizations joined in the campaign to reduce global hunger. In the twenty-first century, these worldwide groups continue to undertake a huge range of activities, including providing emergency famine relief, conducting agricultural research, expanding nutritional education, and broadening media (publicity) campaigning. The aim is not only to feed hungry people, but also to identify the causes of world hunger.

Ethiopia, 2000: A boy stands near the carcasses of animals during the worst famine and drought in two decades.

DEBATE

Should people in developed countries feel a sense of responsibility about helping people in developing countries?

2: MILLIONS OF HUNGRY PEOPLE

Three-quarters of the world's 840 million hungry people live in rural areas in developing countries, where most of the food is provided by small-scale local agriculture. Small farms are at the mercy of nature. If the annual harvest is a good one, the family eats well and perhaps has a small amount of food left over to sell at the market. Any profits help buy seed or fertilizer for the next year's crop.

Yet, in many regions where this lifestyle prevails, the annual harvest is often not a good one. Many of the least developed countries experience extreme and very changeable weather conditions, especially drought (an extended period with little or no rain).

Natural causes

Droughts often destroy harvests, but floods can also devastate crops. After a very successful harvest in the southern African country of Malawi in 1999, the next year's crops were washed away and flooding drowned many farm animals. Further heavy rains delayed planting in 2001 and severe frosts damaged crops that were ready for harvest. In 2002, the country suffered a harsh drought. As the harvest approached again, the parched land and empty grain bins told their own story.

Flooding that follows heavy rains devastates crops as much as a severe drought. After severe floods in February and March 2000, corn crops rotted in the fields of Mozambique, in Africa.

Experts believe that, in addition to extreme weather conditions, dependence on a single crop is also a significant factor in Malawi's food insecurity. Corn was not a main crop there at the end of the nineteenth century. After several decades of government policies aimed at promoting corn (a valuable export crop), it now makes up 80 percent of the average Malawian's diet.

Poor harvests in 2001 and 2002 forced Malawians to pick and eat the 2003 crop and even their precious stores of seeds before they fully ripened. Other people scavenged for banana roots and wild vegetables. In desperation, some Malawians resorted to stealing from neighbors and digging up each other's crops.

Half of all Malawian men and three-quarters of all Malawian women work in agriculture—depending entirely on the land for their survival. In March 2003, the United Nations World Food Program (WFP) estimated that one in three Malawians was malnourished. The WFP pledged to provide food for about 3.3 million Malawians.

Meanwhile, realizing it faced a humanitarian crisis, the Malawian government—together with the WFP and a number of other nongovernmental organizations (NGOs)—distributed seed and fertilizer during the 2003 planting and growing seasons. Despite heavy flooding in some areas, this action, combined with good rains, significantly improved the 2003 harvest over that of 2002. Nevertheless, despite the many resources directed at solving its food emergency, the situation in Malawi remains extremely bleak.

Four women, one of whom is four months pregnant, risk crocodile attacks while searching for water lily bulbs in the Elephant Marshes in southern Malawi. The bulbs are one of the few remaining sources of food.

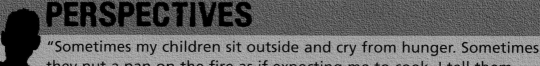

Malawi is not alone. Devastating crop failures occur annually in countries throughout Africa and across other continents, from Bangladesh to Bolivia. The combination of changeable weather patterns and fragile ecosystems often leads to food production emergencies that cause famine.

Human causes

Bad weather rarely creates famine on its own. Weather conditions can make a bad situation worse, however, and can tip a country from crisis into emergency. In the world's most desperate countries, social problems—war, poverty, AIDS, and social inequality—drive the underlying causes of massive starvation and malnutrition.

War and conflict

War tactics changed enormously during the second half of the twentieth century. New conflicts occurred in city streets and village markets with small arms, rather than with heavy artillery on open battlefields, as in World War II. Soldiers not only killed enemy soldiers but also civilians. During the 1990s, conflicts killed two million children, severely injured six million more, and left twelve million children homeless.

Drought affected 31 countries in the early 1980s, but only five (Angola, Mozambique, Chad, Sudan, and Ethiopia) suffered famines. Those five were all in the midst of war. Civil conflicts triggered six of the seven major famines recorded between 1980 and 2000. In 15 of the 44 countries that experienced a food emergency in 2001, conflict was a major cause. War and hunger clearly go hand in hand.

War leads to a general breakdown in law and order. Soldiers may steal food to feed themselves or use so-called "scorched earth" tactics (destroying crops with the aim of starving their enemies into submission). They may deliberately target food

production by bombing farmland, food storage areas, and irrigation systems, and by slaughtering animals and poisoning wells. Alternatively, they may attack agricultural infrastructure by destroying roads and preventing the distribution of fuel, fertilizer, and seed. Cities, ports, and airports may shut down in times of war. A food emergency is often the tragic result.

New conflicts every year also cause about 15 million people worldwide to become refugees, and roughly 22 million others are internally displaced—forced to move within their own countries. At one point during the 1994 war in Rwanda, fought between the ethnic Tutsi and the Hutu, two million Rwandans escaped into neighboring Zaire (now the Democratic Republic of the Congo) in five days—at a rate of 10,000 per hour.

Young militia gunmen in southern Somalia may have added to the country's food crisis in 1993 by preventing the transportation of supplies of fertilizer and seed.

PERSPECTIVES

"Famines are, in fact, so easy to prevent that it is amazing that they are allowed to occur at all."

Amartya Sen, author of Development as Freedom, *1999*

Refugees—people forced from their homes for reasons of personal safety who travel to another country—often escape with little more than the clothes on their backs and whatever possessions they can carry. Refugees have no land, no rights, and no easy access to water and food. Many international organizations, led by the Office of the United Nations High Commissioner for Refugees (UNHCR), provide refugees with emergency aid, especially food, often through refugee camps. In 2000, one in three of those receiving WFP emergency food aid was a refugee (also called a displaced person, or "DP").

Refugees from civil war in Rwanda cross the Rusumo River to Tanzania.

Income poverty

Wherever you are in the world, food costs money. Even a farmer who eats only what he grows needs money to buy

PERSPECTIVES

"Four out of five casualties of the new conflicts are civilians, most of them women and children."

Oxfam Poverty Report, 1995

seeds, fertilizer, and pesticide. People also need to buy any food they cannot grow. They also need food for survival when the crops fail. In the towns and cities of both the developed and the developing world, people grow little or none of their own food, and they must pay for everything they eat.

At the beginning of the twenty-first century, the World Bank ruled that anyone struggling to survive on less than one U.S. dollar a day was officially in the grip of extreme poverty. Currently, about 1.3 billion people in the world fit into this category. Around half a billion children—40 percent of all children in developing countries—live in conditions of extreme poverty.

A typical poor family in the developing world endures a life of hunger, illness, and little opportunity for education. Health care, clean water, and sewage facilities are seldom available. Many of the children who grow up without life's essentials remain poor for their entire lives and they, in turn, raise their own children in poverty.

Twenty-five percent of the world's hungry people are the "urban poor"—very poor people who live in or near a large city. Bad sanitation is often a major cause of disease for the urban poor. This girl stands next to an open sewer in Lucknow, India.

Severe poverty in rural areas of developing nations is driving increasing numbers of people into cities in search of low-level jobs in sweatshops or as servants, or even to scavenge through the waste from richer urban households. A new class of urban poor is being created: families with no farmland on which to grow food and no money with which to buy food. As many as 200 million people living in cities suffer from hunger.

Hunger and poverty are not restricted to poor countries. Large numbers of poor people who cannot afford to pay for a healthy diet also live in the world's richest cities, such as London, England, and Washington, D.C. In these places, the problem is not—as it is in Malawi—the availability of food, but that not everyone can afford to buy it. A supermarket may bulge with food, but what use is that to those who cannot pay for it?

Some argue that hunger and poverty develop under identical conditions. The global AIDS epidemic and social inequality represent two principal causes of modern hunger and poverty.

HIV and AIDS

HIV (Human Immunodeficiency Virus) is the virus that develops into AIDS (Acquired Immune Deficiency Syndrome), a fatal disease that attacks the immune system. In 2003, more than 95 percent of the world's estimated 40 million people infected with HIV/AIDS lived in developing countries.

AIDS is one of the worst humanitarian catastrophes the world has ever faced and is a significant cause of world hunger. Half of all the world's AIDS infections occur in people younger than 25—most of them young parents. By 2003, 14 million children throughout the world became orphans when their parents died because of AIDS. In some areas, an entire generation of young men and women has been severely weakened, leaving the very young and the very old to fend for themselves, without anyone of working age to bring in money and food.

A family affected by AIDS must sell whatever it can to purchase medicine or food. Agricultural production levels fall because the people who would regularly work the fields become too sick to do so. Children leave school so that they can raise food or care for the sick.

Although much poverty and hunger result from government corruption, greed, and cruelty, the same is not true of AIDS.

Homeless people live on the streets of Los Angeles, California, one of the world's wealthiest cities. These two men have little access to the abundant food supplies available in their area.

Governments in Africa and elsewhere have taken steps to fight the disease. Infection rates drop when countries with high percentages of HIV/AIDS patients commit themselves to educating their populations about the disease. If more countries around the world would also enact fair and equal distribution of medicines, even more people would remain healthy enough to raise food and their families.

CASE STUDY

Chantrea is a 38-year-old woman living in Cambodia, which has the greatest number of hungry people in Southeast Asia. Chantrea's fifth child was sickly from birth. Her son never grew properly and died at age two. Chantrea learned after her husband died that he had had AIDS but had been too ashamed to tell her.

Left alone with four children and no money, Chantrea discovered that she, too, tested positive for HIV. She moved to a city to make some money selling fruit on the streets. Her children scavenged in dumpsters for anything they could sell. As each day passed, their hunger worsened.

A local charity that provided support for people living with HIV/AIDS finally stepped in to help Chantrea and her children. The charity supplied food (donated by the WFP), medicines, basic clothing, and shelter. It also encouraged Chantrea to meet other people living with HIV/AIDS and to talk openly about her illness.

An AIDS counselor visits an HIV-positive woman and her children in a slum in Phnom Penh, Cambodia.

PERSPECTIVES

"I was in Malawi and met with a group of women living with HIV. As I always do when I meet with people living with AIDS, I asked them what is their highest priority. Their answer was clear and unanimous: Food."

Peter Piot, Executive Director of the Joint United Nations Program on HIV/AIDS (UNAIDS), 2003

Social inequality

In the world's poorer countries, not everyone is poor. Many people in developing countries manage to feed and clothe themselves and protect their health. In Mexico and Brazil, for example, food availability per person is almost the same as that in Europe. Yet 23 percent of Mexico's people—and 30 percent of those in Brazil—live below the poverty line.

In agricultural communities, there is a direct link between the amount of land owned and the risk of poverty and hunger. In Bangladesh, more than half of landless rural households live in extreme poverty, while only 10 percent of families owning more than 7.5 acres of land live below the poverty line.

A subsistence farmer in the Sahel, an arid region across western north-central Africa, struggles to grow his crops on the poor, rocky land.

In many developing countries, landowners allow tenant farmers to live on and cultivate the land in exchange for rent or part of their harvest. These peasant farmers work hard to farm the land but will never own it. They are at the mercy of the landowners, who may raise rents, demand a greater share of the produce, or force them to move.

In the mid-1970s the Sahel, an area that stretches across Africa from Mauritania to Chad, suffered a terrible famine when harvests throughout the region failed after a long drought. Human actions added to the problem. Sahelian landowners, realizing that hard times lay ahead, sold off much of their good land to large-scale agricultural producers who grew cash crops (crops that are sold—usually overseas—for cash). This practice forced small-scale farmers growing food for local consumption onto unproductive land.

In many developing countries there is inequality on a smaller scale, within communities and families. Not everyone gets a fair share when food is scarce. In many traditional cultures, even though women are the chief family food providers, the females often suffer in favor of the males, who get the best of the food, medical attention, and schooling. Mothers and daughters fill their plates only when father and sons have taken what they want.

In many developing countries, eight out of ten farmers are women. They toil many hours every day tending fruit and vegetables, raising animals, and harvesting crops. In spite of the fact that women throughout the developing world produce 90 percent of all the food, women own only 1 percent of the farmland. UNICEF is particularly concerned about oppressed women, for when mothers suffer, their children usually suffer, too. Giving women more power to feed themselves and to protect the health of their children may help break the cycle of hunger. According to the WFP, seven out of ten of the world's hungry are women and girls.

Members of a women's cooperative cultivate their fields of tomato plants in Masaku, in central Kenya.

PERSPECTIVES

"Wherever women are in control of resources at the family level, in general there is far less malnutrition. Wherever women are oppressed, wherever women are not treated as equals, then you tend to get more malnutrition."

Roger Shrimpton, Senior Nutritionist with Helen Keller International, a UNICEF partner

Global inequality

Finally, inequality that exists between the countries of the world contributes to the hunger problem. At the "global dinner table," some countries heap their plates high, while others scavenge around on the floor for crumbs.

The technological advances of the last century sometimes make us think of the world as a single community, brought closer together than ever before. Modern transportation schedules for aircraft now make a journey across a continent in one day a reality, while at the beginning of the twentieth century, it would take weeks to travel the same distance. And, thanks to the Internet, information crosses the world in an instant.

Yet many inequalities exist within our "global village." The poorest 57 percent (about 3.4 billion people) of the world's population have the same amount of money as the richest 1 percent. The UN ranks the wealth of nations according to a human development index, which takes into account a range of factors, including poverty, education, and life expectancy. In Norway, at the top of the list, life expectancy at birth is

PERSPECTIVES

"Some fifty-four countries are poorer now than in 1990. In twenty-one [countries], a larger proportion of people is going hungry. In fourteen, more children are dying before age five. In twelve, primary school enrollments are shrinking. In thirty-four, life expectancy has fallen."

United Nations Human Development Report, 2003

78.7 years, there is 100 percent literacy, and annual income per person is just under $30,000. At the other end of the scale, a child born in Sierra Leone, Africa, will be lucky to reach his or her thirty-fifth birthday, has a one-in-three chance of learning to read and write, and is likely to have an income of $470 a year.

Ensuring a regular supply of good food, whether in an emergency or not, requires money. In the short term, reliable roads, refrigerated transportation, proper storage facilities, and cash flow are necessary. In the long term, generations of farmers must be educated, supported, and equipped, and the country's economy must be strong and healthy enough to endure depressions without large numbers of people being plunged into poverty—and hunger.

Shoppers in Europe, the U.S., and other developed countries almost always enjoy a wide selection of a wide variety of food.

DEBATE

What are the major causes of world hunger? If you were the head of the United Nations, which one would you tackle first?

3: WORLD FOOD SUPPLY

As we have seen, hunger is not so much caused by a shortage of food as by a lack of access to it. Worldwide food trading practices prevent some people from eating the food they grow. In the early 1990s, about 80 percent of malnourished children in the developing world lived in countries that produced a surplus of food. They went hungry because too much of this food was exported overseas instead of being sold for local consumption.

World supermarket

"Free trade" is a trading system in which the market itself controls what is bought and sold and at what price. Producers sell their goods at the best price they can get and purchasers buy goods at the lowest price they can find.

In this "global market," all countries are supposedly equal partners, with an easy exchange of goods between them. In practice, the free-trade global market is neither free nor fair. The buying power of rich nations greatly outstrips that of the poorest. What happens is that large quantities of food flow out of the developing world and into the developed world, while comparatively little flows in the opposite direction where it is truly needed.

Shelves in a New York City supermarket bulge with food from all over the world.

For instance, although many Peruvians suffer health problems related to low protein intake, much of the high-protein fish caught in the rich Pacific Ocean currents off of Peru's coastline is sold to North American pet food manufacturers. Free market rules dictate that Peruvian producers must find the most profitable outlet for their protein-rich fish. Ironically, if an American pet owner can pay more for cat food than a Peruvian mother can pay for baby food, the cat will get fed and the baby will go hungry.

Fishermen on Lake Titicaca in Peru use traditional methods to catch fish. Twenty-five percent of Peru's population is classified as extremely poor, living on less than one U.S. dollar a day.

The U.S. pet food company pays a minimum price for the raw fish but spends a lot of money while storing, transporting, processing, and distributing the fish. A free market should allow the Peruvian fishermen themselves to earn enough money from the sale of their fish to buy other protein-rich foods. In Peru, excessive government control puts much of the income from the sale of the fish into the hands of the Peruvian government instead. This means that the hoped-for "trickle-down" effect—whereby the money earned from sales would find its way back to the fishermen—is not happening.

The experience of the Peruvian fishermen is very similar to that of farmers across the world. For example, the average banana farmer in Honduras receives only 5 percent of what a shopper in a European or American supermarket pays for a banana. This system keeps the poorest people poor. And, because the market encourages farming for profit rather than for feeding the farmers themselves, many families go hungry.

Coffee beans grow on this plantation in Brazil.

Cash cropping

Poorer countries need to compete with each other, producing food as cheaply as possible in order to keep costs low and attract purchasers. They often do this by specializing in producing food for export. Most food is grown as cash crops for sale abroad rather than for local markets.

Cash crops also tend to be "mono" crops—that is, only one type of food is grown year after year. For example, Honduras in Central America dedicates huge tracts of land to growing bananas. Seventy percent of Honduran export earnings come from bananas, making them a very profitable cash crop. Even if enough of the money trickles down to the farmers, cash-cropping creates financial risks. High market cash-crop prices encourage new producers and more competition. If too much of a certain crop is produced, the market becomes saturated, and prices fall.

Even when cash-cropping makes economic sense, it is not always the best use of land. It can deplete the soil and cause other problem for farmers. By pouring all their efforts into one specific crop, enormous problems arise if insect pests attack or blight affects the crop. Insects can quickly infest an entire area where that single crop is cultivated. Potatoes, grown as a cash crop in many countries, are especially prone to a disease known as late blight. At the end of the 1990s, late blight seriously damaged the potato crop in sub-Saharan Africa and cost the region billions of dollars in export earnings.

Cash crop farmers are taking a great risk by depending so heavily on raising a single commodity for their survival. In October 1998, Hurricane Mitch swept through Honduras. Three days of floods and mudslides pretty much destroyed the banana crop. The environmental damage set back the fragile economic development of Honduras nearly twenty years and plunged millions of Hondurans into deep poverty. The WFP estimates that the post-Mitch reconstruction effort will take many years.

Intensive farming

There is a growing tendency throughout the world for farmers to adopt intensive farming techniques to boost food production (*see pages 35-36*). Although intensive farming offers great financial benefits, it can result in serious environmental harm. Gasoline that fuels agricultural machinery, and poisonous chemicals, such as pesticides, herbicides, and fertilizers can enter the environment. Intensive farming also requires great quantities of water and may deplete supplies and sources of drinking water in countries where water is already scarce.

Soybeans are farmed intensively across the United States. This farm is in Jacksonville, Illinois.

If not properly managed, some farming techniques—chopping down trees to create cropland, lack of crop rotation, heavy grazing by animals—strips away layers of topsoil and turns land into barren, dry desert (a process known as desertification). This process is irreversible and is spreading.

One of the most tragic examples of the environmental dangers of irresponsible farming practices near the Aral Sea—once the world's fourth-largest inland sea—in central Asia. The Aral Sea began shrinking after two rivers that fed the sea were diverted for an irrigation project that provides water for cotton plantations. Now a fraction of its original size, the Aral Sea is a salty wasteland, and its once-thriving fishing ports lie miles from the water's edge. Thousands lost their livelihoods, hunger is widespread, and many people in the area depend on emergency food aid. Chemicals used on the cotton plantations polluted the drinking water. Diseases, such as tuberculosis and cancer, are also common. Although work is underway to slow the rate of shrinking, it is unlikely that life around the Aral Sea will ever return to its former condition.

In the switch to intensive farming methods, developing-world farmers become less self-sufficient. They pay for the high costs involved by striking lucrative deals with international food companies (and often with well-known supermarket chains). These companies buy in such large quantities that they can

A boat lies stranded in Muynak, Russia—once a bustling harbor on the Aral Sea. Irrigation projects diverted two rivers, causing the waters to recede about 60 miles (95 km) in the last half-century.

dictate what is grown, when, and how much they will pay for it. Farmers also depend on the agricultural suppliers who provide better varieties of seed and animal hormones and upon the oil companies that sell the fertilizers and fuels that power the farm equipment.

Subsidies and tariffs

Although the world's richer countries strongly encourage poorer countries to join in the world agricultural markets, they are reluctant to subject their own farmers to the same economic risks.

One reason for this policy is simple: agriculture requires a large workforce, and labor is much cheaper in, say, Africa than it is in Europe. In a truly free market, African countries could produce some crops much more cheaply than in the United States or Europe—causing money losses for farmers in developed countries.

Developed nations protect their farmers in two ways: Their government impose (charge) a tariff, or tax, on food produced by developing countries; and many farmers receive a subsidy (payment) for growing—and sometimes for not growing—a certain crop.

A Texas farmer harvests cotton.

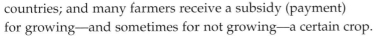

PERSPECTIVES

"Our farmers, who produce . . . cotton 50 percent cheaper than their competitors from developed countries . . . suffer the negative impact of cotton subsidies. These subsidies have caused economic and social crises in African cotton-producing countries. More than ten millions of people in West and Central Africa directly depend on cotton production, and several other millions of people are indirectly affected by the distortion of world market prices due to production and export subsidies . . . our countries are not asking for charity . . . preferential treatment or additional aid . . . Our producers are ready to face competition on the world cotton market—under the condition that it is not distorted by subsidies."

President Blaise Compaore of Burkina Faso, addressing the World Trade Organization, Geneva, Switzerland, June 10, 2003

Subsidies and tariffs protect farmers in developed countries who produce basic crops, such as coffee, sugar, and cotton, that developing countries also produce. For example, Britain subsidizes its sugar beet farmers with $1.6 billion annually. So, even though it costs British farmers (who use heavy machinery, fertilizers, and watering systems) twice as much to produce sugar from beets, AND they receive subsidies from their governments for raising sugar beets, the price of tariff-free British sugar on the international market undercuts the price of the taxed sugar produced by a country like Zambia, Africa.

It may not seem fair that Britain continues to produce sugar. After all, if developed countries bought African sugar instead, many low-income farmers would benefit. But Britain's powerful sugar industry, as well as other food-producing industries throughout Europe, Asia, and the United States, controls prices. And, governments of developed countries traditionally support their agricultural industries because of strong political, historical, and sentimental loyalties to farmers.

The subsidies paid by European and American governments to their farmers are so great that many produce huge food surpluses that never even sell. Annual overproduction of European dairy products amounts to a "mountain" of butter and a "lake" of milk. The WFP and others do what they can

CASE STUDY

Laurent Dumesnil is the last remaining sheep farmer in the Lubéron Mountains in Provence, southern France. He grazes his flock on 36 acres (14.5 hectares) of pasture and sends them off in the summer to wild meadows. This is an expensive method of farming, and Laurent receives financial support from the French government and the European Union (EU) to help him produce his lamb. Although Laurent is a small-scale farmer whose produce makes little impact on world markets, he is worried that the government will bow to pressure to cut all subsidies to farmers. If they do so, the livelihood that supported his father, his father's father, and countless generations before them, will come to an end. He asks, "Why should world trade rules dictate whether French taxpayers can pay me to preserve our way of life and protect our countryside?"

PERSPECTIVES

"We have opened our economy. That's why we are flat on our back."

Sam Mpasu, Malawi's commerce and industry minister, at the WTO Conference, September 2003

to redistribute surpluses to those most in need, but, because most of the food deteriorates quickly, it's a race against time. Wherever possible, the WFP identifies surpluses close to the region with the food emergency.

The World Trade Organization (WTO), which is responsible for overseeing international trade, debated the issue of protectionism at the September 2003 summit in Cancún, Mexico. The poorer countries campaigned for a dismantling of trade barriers and canceling of subsidies. Four West African countries—Burkina Faso, Chad, Mali, and Benin—requested that the United States cut its $3 billion annual cotton subsidy (which totaled more than the value of the four countries' combined harvest) to American farmers. Their request was denied, and 25,000 U.S. farmers shared the $3 billion.

A bumper wheat crop overflows silos in Kansas. Extra grain is piled up outside.

One of the biggest problems with the world food trade is that it places developing-world farmers and developed-world farmers in direct competition with one another. Some experts, particularly those at the World Bank and the International Monetary Fund (IMF), who promote global free trade, argue that competition will drive industries in the developing countries forward. Opponents argue that such competition is unfair to developing-world farmers. As one Sri Lankan activist put it, "free trade is like putting the rabbit and tiger in the same cage."

DEBATE

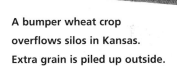

Is it right for governments of developed countries, such as Britain, the United States, and Japan, to protect their farmers with subsidies?

4: FIGHTING BACK

Intergovernmental organizations, particularly offshoots of the United Nations, lead the campaign to turn back the tide of world hunger. The Food and Agriculture Organization (FAO), World Food Program (WFP), the United Nations Children's Fund (UNICEF), the International Fund for Agricultural Development (IFAD), the United Nations Development program (UNDP), and the World Health Organization (WHO) undertake a wide range of activities, including fund-raising, the organization of emergency aid, and research into agriculture, health, and nutrition.

They are supported by a huge number of nongovernmental organizations (NGOs) all over the world, from small, local

On January 25, 1999, an earthquake reduced entire neighborhoods to rubble in western Colombia. The damage rippled through five provinces and devastated more than twenty cities and villages.

specialist organizations to major global campaigners, such as Save the Children, the Red Cross, and the Salvation Army. The cooperation and support of national governments is key to global efforts to relieve poverty and feed the hungry.

Emergency relief

A significant portion of the money spent on relieving world hunger goes toward providing emergency supplies for victims of food emergencies. Natural disasters, such as earthquakes, often trigger these emergencies.

For instance, the most powerful earthquake in a century struck an area of western Colombia in the Andes Mountains on January 25, 1999. Within minutes, 158,000 people lost their homes. There was no electricity, no running water, and no sanitation. The disaster area extended across five provinces in Colombia's coffee-growing heartland. Farmers saw the infrastructure—roads, warehouses, and processing plants—required for their precious cash crop wiped out in an instant.

The Colombian government drew up a national emergency plan and enlisted the help of several international and local NGOs. Governments around the world, from the United States, Europe, Mexico, Japan, and others, donated resources, money, and personnel. Tented villages sprang up throughout the region, and—despite a continual background of civil conflict and unrest—tens of thousands of people received food and medical attention. Within a week of the tragedy, the WFP pledged to feed 115,000 people for six months at a total cost of $4.5 million in U.S. money.

CASE STUDY

With more than two thousand paid workers and up to eighty thousand volunteers, the Colombian Red Cross (CRC) is one of the country's leading NGOs. Immediately after the earthquake, relief workers set up food distribution centers in the disaster area. Emergency aid worker Fernando Betancourt ran the operation in Armenia, one of the worst affected cities. Betancourt stayed in continual contact with CRC headquarters by mobile phone, provided updates on the worsening conditions, and arranged for the efficient distribution of food as quickly as possible.

Betancourt's colleagues in the capital city of Bogotá, Columbia, faced a vexing problem: much of the long route to Armenia went through territory held by rebel armies. Planes carrying food might be shot down. Trucking in supplies also promised difficult and dangerous situations and damaged roads. Furthermore, bandits hoping to get their hands on the cargo made the food shipments vulnerable to attack.

On Friday, January 29, 1999, the first food trucks finally rolled into Armenia. Betancourt and local Red Cross volunteers unpacked the food and stored it in the Red Cross warehouse. Within a week of the earthquake, more than 330 tons (300 tonnes) of rice, beans, lentils, canned tuna, vegetable oil, coffee, sugar, powdered milk, salt, and flour had been distributed. Life changed immensely for most people in Armenia, but the tireless work of Betancourt and his colleagues gave tens of thousands of earthquake victims a second chance.

(Source: Based on documents from the news archives of the International Federation of Red Cross and Red Crescent Societies)

The Columbian earthquake killed about 1,200 people, but quick action by relief agencies prevented even more deaths. And although the 1999 earthquake caused acute, unexpected food supply problems, Colombians are no strangers to social and economic crises. Forty years of civil war have forced 1.5 million people from their homes. About 57 percent of Colombia's population lives in poverty; hunger is a fact of life. Furthermore, armed groups frequently seize food aid (this is common in war-torn countries, such as Sudan, Afghanistan, and Sri Lanka). But, unlike food shortages caused by major earthquakes, Colombia's ongoing food problems do not make dramatic headlines, and millions of people suffer in silence.

Improving agriculture

In the nineteenth and twentieth centuries, industrialized countries experienced something of an agricultural miracle, brought about by the introduction of intensive farming (farming methods that use chemicals and heavy machinery to maximize the productivity of land).

Because of these high-yield farming methods, industrialized countries rarely, if ever, experience food shortages, despite massive increases in population. The Netherlands, for example, one of the most densely populated countries in the world, produces enough food to feed its own population—with about 40 percent left over for export.

During the 1960s and 1970s, organizations combating world hunger focused mainly on improving agricultural methods and particularly on increasing yield (the amount of food produced) in developing countries.

A number of organizations, led by the FAO and IFAD, have campaigned to introduce intensive farming methods to farmers in developing countries. These methods may involve increased use of pesticides and fertilizers, irrigation systems that deliver a constant trickle of water to the soil, and the creation of new

Intensively farmed potatoes grow
In Cornwall In southern England.

varieties of plants that grow faster or bigger or resist disease more effectively.

The Green Revolution

Between 1950 and 1992, world grain production increased by 170 percent—with only a 1 percent increase in the amount of land used to produce that grain. During the 1960s, agricultural scientists developed new high-yield variety (HYV) seeds. The introduction of HYV wheat, rice, and corn to Asian countries made such a dramatic difference that what started as an agricultural experiment soon became known as "the Green Revolution." By 1975, Pakistan and India—threatened by famine in 1965—both produced enough grain to meet the needs of their populations. India established itself as one of the world's biggest agricultural producers when it harvested 144 million tons (131 million tonnes) of grain in 1979.

Those who doubt the benefits of the Green Revolution point out that, despite the increase in food availability per person in India, the number of hungry people in India—more than in any other country in the world—has risen and continues to rise, partly because the increase in grain production has not kept pace with India's rapid population increase. Critics also argue that the higher yields generated by the Green Revolution depend on intensive farming techniques, which come at a high environmental price (*see pages 27-28*).

Fighting malnutrition

A malnourished person may receive enough energy every day (usually from basic carbohydrates, such as cereals and starchy vegetables); however, it is not enough to eat these foods alone. The body also needs regular doses of essential micronutrients, such as vitamins and minerals, to help it perform a range of functions. Oftentimes, it is not the amount—but the type— of food consumed daily that leads to malnutrition.

The planting of genetically modified hybrid maize (corn) seed greatly boosted India's production. Hybrid corn has a greater resistance to a variety of diseases—especially downy mildew—that are particularly damaging to corn crops in southern Asia.

PERSPECTIVES

"While food aid is a tool to support food consumption in vulnerable countries in the short run, in the long run, only improved agricultural performance in these countries can increase their food security."

Shahla Shapouri, United States Department of Agriculture

For instance, a person with a vitamin A deficiency may lose his or her eyesight and may also suffer serious damage to the immune system, leaving the body unable to fight off diseases such as dysentery (which causes severe diarrhea and kills about 2.2 million children a year in developing countries). Vitamin A is found in meat, dairy products, eggs, fruit, carrots, green leafy vegetables, and red palm oil.

In the absence of such foods, just one small capsule—costing a few pennies—provides the correct dose of vitamin A. At the 1990 World Summit for Children, UNICEF committed itself to the virtual elimination of vitamin A deficiency throughout the world by 2010. It set a short-term goal of providing at least one annual supplement for 70 percent of children in affected countries. In 1998, twenty-seven countries achieved the goal. By 2000, forty-three countries were providing at least one dose, and ten of those were providing two annual doses.

Ugandan children wear banners to raise awareness of the need to eat during bouts of diarrhea. Such education campaigns are an extremely important way of spreading basic medical knowledge in developing communities.

Food fortification
Another very successful method of delivering micronutrients to those whose diets are deficient is to add them during manufacturing, usually to a food such as flour. This process is known as fortification.

Iodine is a vital micronutrient that the body needs in tiny but regular doses throughout life. An iodine deficiency (which often occurs in areas with poor soil) can lead to a range of disorders (IDD), including slowed physical growth and some forms of brain damage. Iodized salt (salt fortified with iodine) corrects the effects of an iodine-deficiency diet. Salt serves as the perfect vehicle for importing the minute amounts of iodine everyone's body requires on a regular basis.

Although Switzerland began using iodized salt back in 1922, fewer than 20 percent of households in developing countries were using iodized salt in 1990. This put about 40 million newborn babies at risk of brain damage every year because of their mothers' iodine deficiency. By 2000, however, about 70 percent of households in the developing world used iodized salt. As a result, 91 million children a year were protected from brain damage caused by an iodine deficiency.

Indonesian children test salt for the presence of iodine. In 2002, 65 percent of Indonesian households used iodized salt.

Education

Education is one of the most important weapons in the fight against world hunger. Without education, people lack the

PERSPECTIVES

"Malnutrition is both a consequence and cause of poverty. Children's nutrition and well-being are the foundation of a healthy, productive society."

UNICEF web page, Nutrition: The Big Picture *(www.unicef.org/nutrition/index_bigpicture.html)*

power to change their lives. Yet in 2003, nearly 875 million adults worldwide were illiterate (two-thirds of them women) and 125 million (mostly female) children did not attend school.

Unfortunately, a number of traditional societies believe that girls should remain at home. Twenty-seven million African girls do not go to school, while in southern Asia the number is slightly higher, at twenty-eight million. Yet, as we have seen, more often than not, women rather than men provide food and safeguard the health of their families and communities.

Education programs aimed at combating world hunger take a number of different forms. For example, the FAO teaches farmers and fishermen in developing countries techniques that help them increase their yield. WHO helps fund the education of health professionals, and the World Bank supports programs to teach local food producers business management methods that will improve the general food security of their region.

Micronutrient malnutrition often exists in communities where people do not understand the basic relationship between what

Children learn about nutrition by playing a game at a health clinic in Phnom Penh, Cambodia.

they eat and their health. By supporting health and nutrition education in primary schools throughout developing nations, UNICEF and other aid organizations aim to improve people's knowledge of what is required for a healthy diet.

Breast-feeding

A number of organizations promote campaigns that teach women the importance of breast-feeding. Many uneducated mothers do not realize that breast milk provides babies with all the micronutrients they need for the first six months of their lives. In some countries, aggressive marketing of breast milk substitutes falsely persuades women that artificial formula milk is better for their babies than breast milk. Breast milk is not only extremely nutritious but free, and in most cases, a far better option for a baby.

Several world organizations are working to spread this simple message throughout the villages, schools, and health systems in the developing world. UNICEF estimates that in Brazil the percentage of young babies fed on breast milk alone soared from 4 percent in 1989 to 42 percent in 1996. In Brazil and elsewhere, increases in breast-feeding have reduced infant mortality rates and made countless babies and young children stronger and healthier.

"Triple A"

One key approach to combating malnutrition in the world's poor rural communities is known as "Triple A." This approach aims to empower people with the knowledge to:
- **assess** their nutritional status
- **analyze** what their diet is missing
- take **action** to solve the problem.

For example, a scale and simple weight, height, and age chart help health workers measure and plot the growth of a baby and detect malnutrition before it develops. Continuing support, especially by UNICEF, allows local health authorities in developing countries from the Philippines to Peru to arrange monthly weighing days. Families gather to weigh their babies, discuss their diet, and receive advice—and, if necessary, dietary supplements. Local health workers in each village perform the weighing sessions themselves, canceling the need for highly qualified experts who must travel many miles.

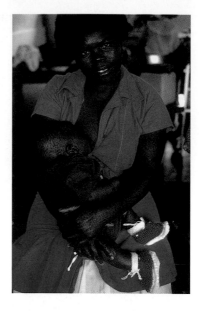

A mother breast-feeding her child at the Queen Elizabeth Centre, near Harare, Zimbabwe.

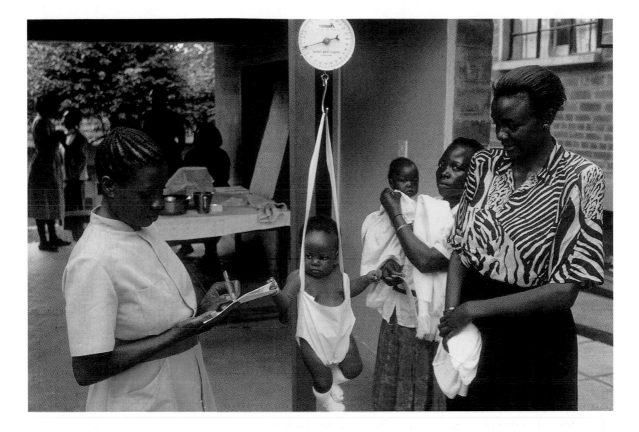

Breaking the hunger cycle

Ultimately, any sustainable (lasting) solution to the world's hunger problem must involve the hungry people themselves. An emergency food package may last a week or even a month, but when that runs out, the risk of hunger may remain as great as ever. High-tech farming machinery for the villagers living on a Cambodian hillside may increase production, but if it breaks down, who will fix it? The best way to permanently break the cycle of hunger and poverty in developing countries is by supplying the local communities with the tools for learning and using proper farming techniques and by providing nutritional education for families.

A local health worker records a child's weight at Rubaga Hospital, Kampala, Uganda.

DEBATE

If an earthquake destroyed part of your country, how would people cope? Would they be in danger of starvation?

5: WHAT THE FUTURE HOLDS

Between 1990 and 2002, the number of hungry people in the world fell by 2.5 million a year. Some nations, particularly China and other Asian countries, made rapid progress. Yet the rate of progress is still too slow to meet the World Food Summit goal of halving world hunger by 2015, set in 1996. In fact, it may take much longer because the human population keeps increasing every year—especially in developing countries. Although a few countries can claim significant gains in combating hunger, their success masks a worsening world situation: Since 1990, the number of undernourished people in the developing nations increased by 80 million.

Although the number of hungry people in the developing world (red line) is falling at a steady rate, it is not fast enough. At current rates, the World Food Summit's target (brown line) set in 1996, will miss its mark, leaving about 200 million people hungry.

Number of undernourished people in the developing world compared with the World Food Summit target

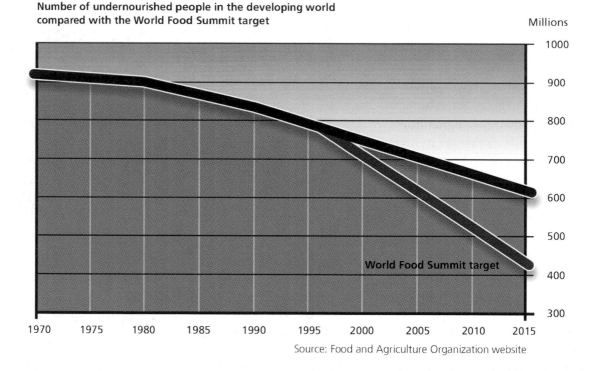

Source: Food and Agriculture Organization website

PERSPECTIVES

"The reasons people go hungry are not mysterious. Mass starvation is not an act of God. Hunger is created and maintained by human decisions. . . . What has been done by some can be undone by others if they use their own strength."

Susan George and Nigel Paige, Food for Beginners, 1986

PERSPECTIVES

"The peace we seek, founded upon decent trust and cooperative effort among nations, can be fortified, not by weapons of war, but by wheat and cotton; by milk and wool; by meat; and by timber and by rice. These are words that translate into every language on earth."

Dwight D. Eisenhower, U.S. president, 1953–61

What can governments do?

At the 1992 Earth Summit in Brazil, industrialized (developed) countries pledged to devote 0.7 percent of their annual income to Overseas Development Aid (ODA). Ten years later, only five nations met this target. (The United States gave 0.12 percent, while England gave 0.3 percent.) Putting a complete end to world hunger could cost $25 billion a year. Although that sounds like a lot of money, industrialized countries' governments spent $300 billion supporting their own agriculture, and consumers in these countries spent $100 billion on cigarettes.

A grass-roots movement promoting organic farming methods signals a growing distaste for large-scale industrial farming in developed countries. Multinational food producers could respond to this trend by using farming techniques that safeguard the environment and protect the interests of developing-world farmers. Increased market opportunities for Fair Trade products, whose producers guarantee that the maximum possible profit goes into the pockets of small-scale farmers, also helps developing nations. Yet Fair Trade and organic products are generally more expensive than the alternatives, and they attract only a fraction of the world market.

The World Bank, the largest source of financial assistance to developing countries, has its headquarters in Washington, D.C.

CASE STUDY

German biologist Ingo Potrykus began developing genetically modified (GM) cereals in the 1970s. By the 1990s, Potrykus led the team that developed "golden rice," a variety of rice fortified with vitamin A. Half of the world's population depends on rice as the mainstay of its diet (many eat little else). Potrykus felt that, if more developing countries would grow vitamin A-fortified rice, it would prevent the starvation of about one million children every year.

By 2004, fourteen golden-rice institutions were set up across southern Asia, but Potrykus and his team had trouble persuading growers to cultivate the controversial GM rice. A number of international organizations argued that golden rice was not an adequate solution to the problem of vitamin A deficiency (VAD). The organizations believed that the real problem was that poverty had restricted people's diets to rice and little else. They believed that providing people with a more varied diet that included the essential micronutrients would better solve the problem.

Vitamin A is important for sight, immunity to disease, growth, and normal development. VAD is a major cause of blindness, especially among children, and it also worsens the effects of measles, diarrhea, and respiratory illnesses. In 2002, the World Health Organization estimated that improved vitamin A nutrition in the developing world could prevent 1.3 to 2.5 million deaths each year among children younger than five years.

Nevertheless, genetic modification remains extremely controversial. One of the chief concerns is that GM crops with built-in pesticides could escape from farmers' fields and turn into "superweeds." Opponents also fear that the GM crops could breed with and change traditional crops or harm wildlife that may eat the GM plants. Opponents also argue that research into the human health benefits from eating GM crops remains unconvincing. Ingo Potrykus's vision remains unfulfilled.

What can the individual do?

Simply by reading this book, you are showing an interest in world hunger. You may even take steps to do something about it. If so, tell other people your opinions. Read stories that relate to world hunger on the Internet or in newspapers, as well as in other books on the subject. (*See page 47.*)

Do not take your food for granted. Next time you go into a supermarket, read the label on each food item. Where is it from? Who grew it? How did it get from the farm to the shelf? Suggest that the store carry more organic products or Fair Trade foods. Write to your local supermarket chain and ask them how they buy their food. If you think they need to consider changing their purchasing practices, tell them so. If you know any local businesspeople, ask if their companies support any food banks.

Find out from politicians how they might use their influence and position to benefit the world's hungry people. If you think they could do more, let them know. Their job, after all, is to listen to people like you.

Finally, do not underestimate the power of younger people to make a difference. By committing yourself now, you may achieve many goals in your lifetime and help make the world a better place.

A Zimbabwean schoolgirl enjoys her lunch. Will the global community ever find a way of ensuring that all the world's people are well nourished?

DEBATE

Is there anything you can do about world hunger?

GLOSSARY

acute hunger the most severe form of hunger; results from a diet deficient in protein, vitamins, and other micronutrients. An acutely hungry person lacks more than 400 food calories daily.

cash crop a crop grown for money rather than for feeding a family.

chronic hunger the most widespread type of hunger; caused by a diet deficient in one or more important nutrients. Chronic hunger victims lack between 100 and 400 food calories every day, sometimes for years.

desertification the process that turns fertile land into desert.

developed (industrialized) country a country with a stable, mostly educated population and an economy based on industry, manufacturing, and other businesses.

developing country a poor country with a growing (and often uneducated) population and an economy based mainly on agriculture.

drought an extended time period with little or no rain.

ecosystem a community of plants and animals that, together with its environment, functions as a balanced, self-sustaining unit.

fertilizer a substance, such as manure or chemicals, that provides crops with nutrients that strengthen them and boost their growth.

food insecurity an inconsistent food supply that causes large numbers of people to suffer from hunger, undernourishment, and starvation.

intensive farming agricultural techniques designed to increase the productivity of land by using complex machinery, expensive chemicals, and fewer workers.

malnutrition a general term for the range of conditions that result from a diet deficient in essential proteins, vitamins, or minerals.

micronutrient a tiny quantity of an essential component, such as vitamin A, iodine, and iron, found in a healthy diet.

mono crop a single crop planted over a large area in which no other crops are planted.

pesticide a chemical—usually a poison—that controls, repels, or kills pests, such as insects, weeds, and some birds, that damage plants.

protectionism an economic policy that protects the markets of a given country. A government may protect its own producers (that is, ensure that they sell their products for a reasonable price) by subsidizing production costs or by placing tariffs on foreign goods.

stela a stone pillar or a slab engraved with words, pictures, or symbols that describes an event.

subsidy a payment, usually by a government, to farmers or other manufacturers of goods, that helps regulate the price of a particular commodity and keeps that product competitive on the market.

tariff a tax imposed on goods when they enter or leave a country.

transition country a country, such as one of those in Eastern Europe and the Baltic countries formerly belonging to the Soviet Union, that is making the transition from a planned economy to a free-market economy, like those found in the United States and Western Europe.

undernourishment a daily intake of food that averages 200 Calories less than what a healthy diet should contain.